Tools for Better Communication

Pete Thompson, LCSW & Lynne Thompson

Tools for Better Communication

Pete Thompson, LCSW
&
Lynne Thompson

ISBN: 979-8-218-65667-6

CONTENTS

INTRODUCTION

Fantasyland

Disney animation feature movies are famous for bringing us the 'happily ever after' stories, from Snow White and Sleeping Beauty, who were awakened by the kiss from a handsome prince to Cinderella rescued from abuse (also by a prince), toting a glass slipper. The only problem with these fairy tales is that in real life, the *'happily ever after'* part is supposed to continue long after the credits roll, with two very different people living together. Unfortunately, that part of the script gets very messy, and the characters often go on strike or walk out altogether.

It only takes the newly married couple two years, or less, to realize life is not a fairytale. Each person comes into the relationship with his or her own set of values and traditions. For example, some families open their Christmas gifts on Christmas Eve, while others open them on Christmas Day. Which one will you honor? Which side of the family will partake in your celebration?

When you really, truly, get to know a person, you discover that he or she believes and does things very different from what you call normal. This realization is followed by an effort to transform the other person to the *normal way* of doing things. Naturally, conflicts arise when both spouses attempt to encourage, coax, or force their own ideas, traditions, or behaviors upon the other. This can lead to battles (often referred to as fights) about who wins and gets his or her own way. This suggests there is a winner and loser. But what does God want?

Are there ways to communicate and work through

differences and reach a peaceful agreement? Is there a path forward to the promise of Genesis 2:24,

> *"For this reason a man shall leave his father and his mother, and be joined to his wife; and they shall become one flesh."*

As a biblical therapist for thirty-five plus years, who has counseled thousands of couples and walked them through the conflict process, I can assure you there is a way forward to happily ever after. It begins with what I call Tools.

Tools For Successful Communication

I've been to many historical sites over the years. I've visited Williamsburg, Virginia, one of the early colonial settlement sites in the United States. I've walked through Spanish Missions along the California coast and even explored Indian ruins in the deserts of Arizona. Most of these sites boast fabulous museums, with exhibits featuring ancient findings, including tools, lots of tools: tools for building, tools for carving, tools for blacksmiths and farm use, tools for meal preparation, tools for textiles, and tools for weaponry. Without these early implements ancient life would have been more difficult. It's no wonder that tools are the key to modernization.

Today's tools look different but are nonetheless just as crucial for our survival. Current tools look like automobiles, tractors, gas stoves, and mechanical assembly lines. Many of our tools rely upon things we can't even see like the internet, or fiber cables in the ground. A life without tools, then and now, makes living on earth very difficult. But merely possessing tools is not enough, for tools to be useful you need to know how to use them correctly. A tool is only as useful as the user's understanding of it.

Some have asked why I came up with the concept of tools as a delivery system for mental health concepts. As a guy who is occasionally called upon by his wife to fix things, I've learned the importance of tools. They help me carry out tasks on that never ending honey-do list. I'm reminded of sage words from my father, "You can use your brain, or you can use your back," and tools are the brain that saves you time, sweat, and pain. It is better to use a wrench to loosen an oil plug, than using your fingers. Even household tasks are made easier with tools: vacuum cleaners, dishwashers, electric mixers, and beadmakers make short work for what our ancestors took all day to accomplish.

So how does the concept of tools relate to mental health and relationships? I have seen couples over the years who are clearly trying to achieve their goals but lack the tools necessary for success. It's painful to watch. If they'd only had the proper tools. People usually come to counseling because they have tried to resolve a problem or situation that seems unsolvable. They have exhausted their own resources and find it doesn't work. The result is needless pain that can be avoided or addressed with the proper tools. By tools, I mean introducing new ways of thinking, and new behaviors that will help them achieve their desired outcome. And rather than keep these time-tested tools to myself, I want to explain them to as many people as possible for healing to occur in the household of faith.

I am a biblical therapist, I believe the best tools offered can be found in God's Holy Word, the Bible. The infinite resources found in the scriptures are more than adequate for bringing peace and healing into relationships. It's more than just reading the Bible every day, although that is imperative for change to come, but rather to interject those biblical precepts into daily life. It's not easy, and many people struggle with past experiences and decisions that deter them from the healing God desires in their life.

As a cognitive behavioral therapist, I was trained to understand that bad behavior, dysfunctional emotions, and irrational beliefs are a byproduct of ideas that need to be modified or changed to have healthy outcomes. Bad ideas need to be replaced by good ones. This type of psychotherapy conforms with scripture's idea of thinking as expressed in 2 Corinthians 10:5,

We are destroying speculations and every lofty thing raised up against the knowledge of God, and we are taking every thought

captive to the obedience of Christ...

I have seen many marriages struggling with destructive thinking, but high up on the list is the way they think about, and practice, communication. My desire for *Tools for Better Communication-* is to help deliver new tools, in hopes they'll offer you new ways to think about how you interact as a couple. I want to help you demolish arguments and pretensions that put you at odds with what God has planned for your marriage. I want to show you a new way to embrace helpful thoughts so that together you can become obedient to Christ and enjoy his good plan for your marriage. I invite you to join me in discovering various tools that bring clarity and understanding, leading to a strong marriage. For some of you this will be an opportunity to build on an already strong and growing relationship, for others this is an answer to what might seem like an unfixable situation.

At the end of each section there are interactive questions and a call to action, useful for therapy sessions, group study, and personal implementation. Regardless of how you plan to use this resource, I want to thank you for having the bravery in embarking on something new. I believe these tools offer steps to better communication, fostering peace and healing that ultimately glorifies God.

Questions

1. What do you define as 'happily ever after?'
2. Have you ever seen 'happily ever after?' Explain why you think it can or cannot exist.
3. What things did you grow up with that you consider normal but are different from your spouse?
4. What kinds of physical tools do you use at home? How do your tools make life easier?
5. Why do you think couples struggle with communication?

Call to Action

As you delve into healthy ways to communicate, take time to pray, asking God to open your heart and mind to receive what lessons He has instore for you.

CHAPTER ONE – SCAR TISSUE

Before I begin to share some communication tools, I need to explain the *why* behind its purpose. The reason *why* marriages, and people in general, get stuck in bad responses. The reason why this takes time and patience. The reason why your response is crucial to a successful outcome. Let me explain:

I used to work as a trauma social worker in an emergency room back in California, some thirty years ago. It was my job to act as a mediator between the doctor and the patient's family. I learned a lot working closely with doctors. I remember one time a physician shared his frustration trying to set up an intravenous (IV) drip on a patient addicted to drugs. I asked him why it would be so hard. After all, he had lots of injection site marks on his arms; couldn't you just pick one? The doctor explained that injections in those spots caused scar tissue to develop, creating a Kevlar-type surface over the skin. This man's continued drug injections in those areas made his skin almost impenetrable for future needles.

Similarly, communication styles can develop barriers or scars that are just as tough to break through. Even good communication, like the IV medicine, is difficult to administer due to the emotional scar tissue built up over time. I call this "Emotional Scar Tissue" or EST.

What is EST?

Each time we are angry or frustrated we have the potential to share harsh words or behaviors with another person. This causes pain in a person's mind, and since we as humans are pain adverse, we develop ways to protect ourselves from hurting that way again. People respond to the words and/or behaviors by developing an emotional patch or scar that keeps them from feeling that way again. If more emotional attacks continue, that person may grow numb or develop a cold heart toward the individual. Eventually, trust is broken, and the relationship stays distant or ends.

This is what I see when married couples come to me regarding communication failures. They have continued to push each other's buttons to the point where they avoid discussing any topic that might become problematic or turn into conflict. Eventually, the lists of topics become so numerous they stop talking altogether. As couples try to protect themselves from EST, even the healthy parts of the relationship begin to erode. This loss of connection and intimacy creates distance, ultimately causing the relationship to fail.

The relationship failure is not isolated to just marriage. Family, friendships, and even casual relationships suffer when EST has created a lack of trust, and the belief that communication is not safe. In casual relationships EST is expressed in ways that have less impact on our long-term interaction but can nonetheless present problems. Let me give you an example.

When I was twenty-one years old my father gave me a set of golf clubs. I hated golf. But to show that I wasn't totally ungrateful for the gift, I signed up for golf as my elective in junior college. It was there I was able to fully demonstrate my lack of motivation for the game. I just didn't care, and it showed. My teacher pulled me aside one day and called me out, asking why I signed up at all. I explained the gift and then expressed my desire to fulfill my PE requirement since I planned to graduate at the end of the semester.

The teacher then explained the golf class didn't fulfill the requirement to graduate. I panicked. I asked if I could take another class that would fulfill the requirement. The coach said there was room in the racquetball class but questioned why he should trust me to perform any better considering my poor motivation in golf.

In this embarrassingly true story, it is clear, I left my poor teacher with some emotional scar tissue. He didn't want to continue in any type of future relationship based upon my bad behavior. Happily, this teacher showed me grace and allowed me to redeem myself in another class (which I did). But in familial and marriage relationships, the stakes are higher, occurrences of scar tissue are more frequent, and the consequences often more devastating.

Sure, I almost didn't graduate on time, but losing a marriage is too high of a price to pay. I once heard a pastor say, "Everyone is a preacher, you preach who you are and what your message is with everyone you meet." There are opportunities to inflict EST on everyone you encounter; it's a universal problem.

Doesn't Everyone Have EST?

Yes, we all have experienced bad responses by people around us due to sin. Even though the sin of others may not have come as a direct verbal or physical attack against you personally, the consequences of people's sinful decisions have a wide-reaching impact. As children, our earliest painful memories with our family can result in EST. Children observe how other people act in public and in private behind closed doors. When people they trust, respond in destructive ways, trust is broken. This affects future relationships becoming impaired and underdeveloped. Children will often seek support outside the family system which can be good or bad. One of the consequences of early EST is children developing a negative worldview, hampering future success.

In case you think that Emotional Scar Tissue is something new, you'd be wrong. There are events throughout history that demonstrate EST in people's lives. Even in biblical history. Let's look at two:

One example of emotional scar tissue comes from 1 Samuel 25:4-35. King David is taking asylum in the wilderness, when he requests resources from Nabal, a nearby farmer. David's men had been a protection for his shepherds for quite some time, so the request was legitimate. Nabal's response to the request not only left emotional scar tissue but pricked David's past scars:

"Who is David? And who is the son of Jesse? There are many servants today who are each breaking away from his master. Shall I then take my bread and my water and my meat that I have slaughtered for my shearers, and give it to men whose origin I do not know?" - 1 Samuel 25:10-11

Did Nabal know who King David was? Evidently, he did, since he knew David was the son of Jesse. By commenting on servants breaking away from their masters, Nabel revealed he was aware of David's plight- fleeing from the angry King Saul, whom God had rejected as king over Isreal. All those comments were meant to harm David with EST, hitting David where he was most vulnerable. David's response to EST was to destroy the household of Nabal, until a wise woman (the wife of Nabal) brought healing balm to the situation. She replied,

"The Lord your God will certainly make a lasting dynasty for my lord, because you fight the Lord's battles, and no wrongdoing will be found in you as long as you live. Even though someone is pursuing you to take your life, the life of my lord will be bound securely in the bundle of the living by the Lord your God, but the lives of your enemies he will hurl away as from the pocket of a sling." – 1 Samuel 25:29-31

Abigail both acknowledged David's rightful title as King and honored his many battles, including the destruction of the mighty Goliath with a sling. Her ability to calm the situation by working against inflicted EST saved her and her entire household.

Another example of EST is found in the book of Job. In an effort to explain the unexplainable, Job's friends took it upon themselves to educate Job about his suffering.

Remember now, who ever perished being innocent? Or where were the upright destroyed? According to what I have seen, those who plow iniquity And those who sow trouble harvest it. By the breath

of God they perish, And by the blast of His anger they come to an end. - Job 4:7-9

During Job's time of great anguish his friend has arrived to tell Job the only reason you are suffering is because you did bad stuff. Nice. Not only is the friend inflicting EST, but it's not true.

This passage shows us that many times our own lack of understanding can bring Emotional Scar Tissue into another's life. Fortunately, for Job, it was God who eventually restored him with healing, wealth, and the grace to forgive his friends.

Bad Responses to EST

As seen in the biblical passages above there are negative ways to act in response to EST. In David's case he initially sought revenge; In Job's case he questioned the goodness and authority of God. EST is not dormant; left untreated, it requires a response. Some of these responses keep us from moving forward while others can be deadly.

A common negative long-term effect of EST is isolation. Because EST doesn't just come from one incident or perhaps even one source, the individual with untreated EST will decide that people in general cannot be trusted or allowed into his or her life. When difficulties come and it would be beneficial to reach out for help, the reticent sufferer decides that the risk is too great and instead retreats from all relationships. Just like the IV addict with Kevlar skin, their inability to receive good care hampers their ability to emotionally heal. This person who has shut out everyone is now vulnerable to even worse scenarios.

The evil one, Satan, is most successful in a person's life when all lifelines have been cut off. Scripture warns us about not neglecting fellowship with other believers. Hebrews 10:25 reads,

> *"not forsaking our own assembling together, as is the habit of some, but encouraging one another; and all the more as you see the day drawing near."*

Although this verse is great for incentivizing people to attend church, the "why" behind the message is crucial. Words like: "encouragement" and especially as "the day draws near", communicates the importance of a support system, especially as hard times escalate in the future. Ecclesiastes 4:12 reminds us that a lone wolf is vulnerable,

> *"And if one can overpower him who is alone, two can resist him. A cord of three strands is not quickly torn apart."*

The cord refers to you, another believer, and God.

Another bad response to EST is the 'pay it forward' effect. It's true that hurt people hurt people. Those who suffer from unresolved EST can give EST to other people. It's the pain that keeps on giving. Consequently, inflicting others with the same pain you received does nothing to permanently resolve your own pain. We inflict pain because EST taints our water source. There may be no intention of you or anyone else purposely inflicting pain on someone else, but because of personal pain this is all you have to offer right now. Until that wound can be healed by a relationship with God, the well will keep delivering tainted water.

Lastly, sometimes people adopt harmful addictions to cope with the pain. These addictions are a distraction to numb the pain we've experienced. When EST is triggered, it's normal to run to something to distract from the pain; examples include alcohol, drugs, porn, food, materialism, or chasing a new relationship. All of these are low hanging fruit for the enemy to trap people, even believers, in addictive and dangerous behavior, instead of addressing the problem and working through it.

The Solution

People can spend lots of years and money trying to chase the latest therapeutic intervention to address the results of EST in their lives. But there is one solution more effective than anything our human strength can toss at the problem, It's forgiveness. Before I explain let me be clear, this occurs *after* you have placed yourself in a safe, non-threatening environment, then the next step is your personal healing. Forgiving those who introduced EST is imperative. Why? There are a few important reasons.

First, God in his word has commanded us to forgive.

Be kind to one another, tender-hearted, forgiving each other, just as God in Christ also has forgiven you. - Ephesians 4:32

Secondly, because the Bible explains it's conditional.

But if you do not forgive others, then your Father will not forgive your transgressions. Matthew 6:15

Seems harsh right? Let me help you with the process. Many of you have watched or attended court trials. Usually, there is a judge, a jury, the accused, and the victim. The judge's role is to interpret and apply the law, so justice is served. For this to happen, it must be impartial. Meaning, you can't say to one person "you are guilty" of an action and then turn around and tell another person who is guilty of the same thing, "you are not guilty." That would be a miscarriage of justice.

God is the judge and his standard for compliance to the Law is perfection. Unfortunately, no one can meet that standard. Jesus once told a story that illustrates this very idea. In the parable of the unforgiving servant, Matthew 18:23-35, Jesus shares about a slave who owed the King a debt he couldn't repay. But the King felt compassion for him and released him from the debt. Then the servant proceeded to go after a fellow slave and demand he repay a debt. But there was no compassion, rather he had his fellow man tossed into debtor's prison. The King was angry, and had the unforgiving servant tortured until he could repay the debt. The slave hadn't followed the King's example of compassion and forgiveness.

There is something that arises in us when we forgive others. We start to see them as we see ourselves, broken people who can't make things perfect on this side, no matter how hard we try. We don't deserve God's forgiveness, yet we ask for it. How can we not extend it to others who are equally poor and wretched? The truth is we have all brought EST into someone's life, intentionally or not. We have been the perpetrator as much as we've been the victim. God is clear about how forgiveness works:

Whenever you stand praying, forgive, if you have anything against anyone, so that your Father who is in heaven will also forgive you your transgressions. Mark- 11:25

Lastly, forgiveness breaks the cycle of hurt, and introduces God's pay it forward system of grace and kindness. This is God's answer to emotional scar tissue. We are imprisoned when we hold onto the EST that God wants to heal. By forgiving we are not saying that EST is okay; we are saying that God wants so much more for us. Unresolved EST continues the cycle of hurt and keeps us from the fellowship of other believers. Forgiving and moving forward opens a whole new world of grace-filled living, where you can love broken people, like yourself.

The Good Fight

Now that I've explained EST, one of the goals when having a discussion/conflict is to not inflict more EST upon your spouse or anyone else. As I've explained, unhealthy discussion presents a barrier to solutions and you both lose. Name calling, belittling, swearing, or aggressive behavior has no place in Christian conflicts. God calls us to a higher standard as we pursue righteousness. The Proverbs offer wisdom about how we should and should not handle conflict. In Proverbs 15:1,

"A gentle answer turns away wrath, / But a harsh word stirs up anger."

In Proverbs 15:18,

"A hot-tempered man stirs up strife, / But the slow to anger calms a dispute."

Regardless of how things used to be during past conflicts, it's important to move forward by practicing a new way of conversing that keeps EST at bay. Paul says it best in Colossians 3:7-9:

"You used to walk in these ways, in the life you once lived. But now you must also rid yourselves of all such things as these: anger, rage, malice, slander, and filthy language from your lips. Do not lie to each other, since you have taken off your old self with its

practices." (New International Version)

Today is a new day with a fresh start toward healthy communication. With this in mind, let me introduce some tools that build healthy communication strategies into your relationship.

Questions

1. Can you think of a time in your life when you experienced EST?
2. How did you cope with it?
   - Avoidance
   - Introducing behaviors to numb the pain
   - Developing ways to get even
   - Shutting down and becoming isolated
3. What was the natural response you had when you ran into someone who gave you EST in the past?
4. Can you recall EST experiences as a child? Did it affect your relationship with that person? How?
5. Has there ever been a time when you said or did something to someone you later regretted? What happened?
6. Name an instance when you might have given someone EST, intentionally or accidentally.
7. Can you think of an instance where you felt disrespected like Nabal's interaction with King David? What emotions came to the surface?
8. Share an instance when you had an Abigail in your life who helped you not act on bad impulses?
9. In the case of Job's friends, we see bad doctrine can give EST. Have you had experiences with bad doctrine that caused you EST?
10. Can you think of other bible characters that gave EST to each other?
11. Share a time when you pushed everyone out of your life and felt cut off.
12. Have you ever been a lifeline to someone who is isolated?
13. Do you ever recall a time when your pain, due to EST, vented all over someone else? How did that go?
14. Is there a time in your life when you demanded somebody to account for what they did to you?
15. Have you always accounted for something wrong you did

to someone else?

16. How does God pay grace forward in your life?

Call to Action

Take a moment of silent prayer and ask God who you need to forgive that has given you EST. Next, ask God to recall people you have given EST to.

CHAPTER TWO – WAITING TOOL

A Tale of Two Cakes: Story #1

Once upon a time there was a husband who was given a lovely birthday party by his wife. All his friends attended, and a good time was had by all, then came time for the best part…the cake. After blowing out the candles, slices were served, and the husband noticed it was a carrot cake, which was okay but not his favorite. He wondered why his wife didn't remember to purchase his favorite kind of cake, as she always had before. Perhaps there was a good explanation. But instead of confronting her at the party he went back to the celebration as if nothing was wrong. Throughout the night, he thought of asking her on the matter but sensed from God this was not a good time to do so. Just as the couple was about to turn in for the night, his wife volunteered, "Hey I'm sorry about the cake, I called several bakeries last week and all of them said they couldn't make your favorite. Something about supplies. But I promise to get you that cake as soon as they come in. I hope you weren't too disappointed."

A Tale of Two Cakes: Story #2

Once upon a time there was a husband who was given a lovely birthday party by his wife. All his friends attended, and a good time was had by all, then came time for the best part…the cake. After blowing out the candles, slices were served and the husband noticed it was a carrot cake, which was okay but not his favorite. He wondered why his wife didn't remember to purchase his favorite kind of cake, as she always had before. Was she mad at him? Trying to make a point of some kind? Had he done something wrong? He marched into the kitchen and confronted his wife, "What is wrong with you? Are you trying to make a point or something? You know my favorite cake and you purposely didn't get it? Thanks for nothing!" His wife proceeded to deliver the remainder of the cake with a direct hit to his face. The party ended early, and he spent the night in the guestroom.

Assessment

Two stories, two different outcomes with communication in each making all the difference. Relationships are complicated, and just like a cake that has several components: ingredients, mixing, and baking, all must be included, or the outcome can end in a mess. In this instance, the important component is time. In story #1 we see that the husband practiced restraint in confronting the issue of the wrong cake. He figured there was most likely a logical explanation why his favorite cake didn't make it to the party. He figured he didn't have all the information needed to determine a proper response. Rather than rely on his carnal desire to know why, he relied upon the prompting of the Holy Spirit to wait for the best time. The husband in story #2 lacked that spiritual discernment. This husband demanded an immediate explanation. He made assumptions, jumped to conclusions, and shot accusations that weren't supported by facts. Additionally, he devalued any effort that had been put forth by the wife. His communication resulted in difficult consequences that led to other unfortunate events.

Waiting is not easy. We live in an instant culture. I remember as a child back in the 70s good things took time. Television shows were anticipated days ahead, since they only ran once, and hunting for that perfect school outfit meant visiting several department stores. Let's face it, we are fast food, Amazon Prime, and Door-Dash culture. It only makes sense we fail to demonstrate waiting well, when it is hardly ever practiced in our daily life. Not practicing patience short circuits our ability to wait for the truth. We are caught in the tyranny of the immediate, which doesn't leave time for clarity to fully understand why things turned out the way they did. The desire to hurry into things, or assumptions like those in the story, doesn't give time for evaluating motives or checking for comprehension, to see if the person even correctly heard what was said. Waiting is a valuable communication tool. Things are not always as they appear so rushing to conclusions prohibits good communication.

Practicing Love

Another communication crusher is lack of love. Love takes time. If you read 1 Corinthians 13, often called the love chapter, you'll see how beneficial love can be in communication, and actually establishes a template for waiting and patience, seasoned with grace. Let's review a few of the verses in light of the Two Cakes stories.

1 Corinthians 13 Love Attributes	Our Two Cakes Template
Love is patient	Waiting to address an issue in its proper time and allowing all the information to be revealed.
Love is kind	Kindness doesn't desire to degrade or belittle; words communicated need to be seasoned appropriately.
Love is not self-seeking	It doesn't make demands for the pleasure of self. The focus on "I" in communication makes for a poor foundation for common ground.
Love does not dishonor others; It is not easily angered	Bad communication at its core is used to 'take down' another person, not lift them up.
Love rejoices with the truth	It sometimes takes more than a minute or even a day for the truth to surface.
Love always trusts and hopes	It's better to believe the best of a person until proven otherwise with full disclosure.

Recipe Tips

So which cake story will you exhibit in your communication? How should you respond when things don't seem to add up or aren't fast tracking the way you desire? Here are some recipe tips for avoiding a food fight:

- Find the right time and place for gleaning additional information.
- Make sure you have all the information before judging a situation.
- Be gracious by acknowledging the positive. For example, "I love the fact that you threw me a party. It was so considerate."
- Relay questions and/or statements in a non-accusatory way, "I noticed what happened was different than I expected."
- When there is miscommunication in a situation, take responsibility for your part. "I think I may have jumped to a conclusion before I had all the information. I'm sorry, can you help me understand?"

Questions

1. Times have changed over the years. Can you think of things we used to have to wait for instead of getting instant results?
2. How has our instant culture influenced how we interact with other people?
3. What did patience look like in the cake stories?
4. Have you ever jumped the gun on something and later realized waiting would have resulted in a better outcome?
5. Can you think of another time when you waited and were glad you did?
6. Have you sensed the Spirit of God directing you in a challenging situation?
7. Why do you think it's important to have all the facts before responding to something?
8. Can you think of a time when the truth didn't come out of a situation until later?
9. How would the practice of waiting impact your relationships today?
10. What do you do to season your words with kindness?
11. Why is it so challenging to focus on the needs of others instead of yourself?
12. What is something truthful you could say to your spouse right now that would lift him or her up?
13. Why is truth so important in communication?
14. Why is it so difficult to believe the best in someone?
15. What does love look like according to 1 Corinthians 13?

Call to Action

Practice patience. Notice how you respond when placed in waiting situations, (e.g., waiting for your coffee order, the car to be fixed, waiting for a text response, or standing in line at the grocery store).

CHAPTER THREE – DELIVERY TOOL

The Book

Imagine a couple coming into my office for marital therapy. They notice the comfortable couch, take advantage of the free water and coffee, and settle in for their first session. Both share concerns describing the situation. Then, as a biblical therapist, I decide I want to share a passage of scripture with them pertinent to the topic at hand. But rather than read the passage, or hand them a Bible to look up the passage, I throw the five-pound study Bible right at the face of the husband. He ducts just in time and considers returning the Bible back in the same fashion. Regardless, he knows one thing, he will NEVER again have anything to do with this therapist.

Later they run into to the pastor that referred them to me. "Hey, how did it go with the therapist?" the pastor asks the husband. "He threw his Bible at me!" the man exclaimed. "Well, now," the pastor responded, "I know a lot of counselors who use the Bible to direct people toward good answers." The man grabs and shakes the pastor's shoulders. "No, you don't understand, he actually threw his physical Bible right at my face!" Needless to say, that man, his wife, as well as the pastor will never use my services again.

I use this absurd example to explain how destructive it can be when a good message, even God's word, can be refused based upon a bad delivery. There are many wonderful things that can be shared with a person struggling in life, but whether he or she hears us or not often depends upon a good delivery. When a message is delivered poorly everyone suffers, in my silly story the couple might be hesitant to darken the door of any other biblical counselor, and the counselor might find that his reputation of Bible assault proceeds him, causing him to lose the opportunity to speak truth and healing into another's life. So how do we share truth?

The Tone

Tone is important when we speak to another person. The Merium Webster Dictionary defines *tone* as: "a particular pitch or change of pitch constituting an element in the intonation of a phrase or sentence." Many times, marriage conflicts arise due to statements made in what was perceived as a snarky tone. Common everyday questions like, "What is for dinner?" or "Are you going to wear that?" Can pose serious conflicts when delivered with a confrontational or harsh tone. In scripture we read that,

> *"A gentle word turns away wrath/but a harsh word stirs up anger."* - *Proverbs 15:1.*

For some people who desperately want to be heard, and drive their point home, gentleness might be seen as weakness. This is not true. On the contrary, gentleness is a tool that wields extreme power. In Proverbs 25:15 Solomon, the wisest King ever to lead Israel, proclaims,

> *"By forbearance a ruler may be persuaded, / and a soft tongue breaks the bone."*

In other words, restraining our tone and delivering a message in a gentle fashion has the strength to influence and make the difference, even in challenging circumstances.

Realize the Information is Fresh

The ideas that you are trying to communicate might be new information to the hearer. Remember, it was once new to you at one time. You've had time to process the merits of the information, to test it out and see if you agree with it, and time to weigh the benefits and the costs. It is only fair that you allow ample time for your hearer to do the same.

Sometimes when people question our beliefs and statements, we perceive their response as intimidation or a threat. This is again, not always true. Mature communication allows room for the other person to exercise due diligence by examining all the facts. Remember in scripture we are encouraged to count the cost of our decisions,

"Suppose one of you wants to build a tower. Won't you first sit down and estimate the cost to see if you have enough money to complete it? For if you lay the foundation and are not able to finish it, everyone who sees it will ridicule you, saying, 'This person began to build and wasn't able to finish." - Luke 14:28-30.

Allowing the same time and courtesy to your hearer, as you gave yourself for processing new information, will go far in promoting healthy communication with a lot less stress.

Timing is Everything

At our home we have unofficial non-discussion hours. We don't discuss anything important or something that requires a decision before 8am, at dinner, or after 9pm. Why? It's important to be at our best when receiving information. My wife is not a morning person, and I am not a night owl, so making decisions or confronting a problem isn't well received during those hours. Dinner hour is not for heavy talk but casual topics or the latest news article or Bible lesson learned. An empty stomach is a fertile ground for conflict to arise.

We need to be wise about finding the best circumstances for delivering our message. Busy schedules may require an actual calendar appointment to be made, allowing for ample time to address a difficult topic or a crucial decision. This secures time for the necessary groundwork to prepare for the topic at hand.

Trying on Shoes

When you are presenting information it's important to ask yourself, "How would I like to receive this information?" We are asked by the Lord to, "love your neighbor as yourself," so who is your neighbor? It is everyone including your spouse. Sometimes the grace we give others doesn't match the grace we give to our spouse. One day my wife quipped at me, "Would you talk to your clients this way?" I shot back, "You are not my client." Funny, but not really. I needed to offer my spouse the same patience, kindness, and respect that I offer those who come to my office for help. In fact, even more so, since she is my wife, and I've promised to love her as Christ loves the church.

Before you deliver a message to someone, take that extra second to tell it to yourself first. Are you saying it in the manner you'd like to hear it? If not, shuffle the words around to make them softer. Your listener will be more likely to receive what you have to say.

In conclusion, we want to remember the words of Paul when he exhorted Timothy:

> *"Don't have anything to do with foolish and stupid arguments, because you know they produce quarrels. And the Lord's servant must not be quarrelsome but must be kind to everyone, able to teach, not resentful." - 2 Timothy 2:23-24.*

This includes 'not throwing the book' at someone whether you are discussing a problem, trying to reach a decision, or presenting the truth. If you take the time and put forth the effort to practice good communication, I can't guarantee that the person will see things your way, but at least the rejection won't be based upon your delivery, but the message itself.

Questions

1. What would you have done if the Bible was hurled at you?
2. Can you recall a business that lost customers because of the way communication was handled?
3. Have you ever been part of a conversation where the person probably had a good idea but shared it so poorly you could not listen to it?
4. How did that affect your future relationship with that person?
5. When have you been accused of using the wrong tone?
6. How did it affect how the person heard your message?
7. When were you unable to hear a message due to a bad tone?
8. How did you initially want to respond to the message given with a bad tone?
9. What happens in your mind when you receive new information? How do you process it?
10. Why would a person need time to process information?
11. Is there a time of day or situation where you are not receptive to new information?
12. In what ways have you learned the importance of timing when delivering a message?
13. Is there a time when you spoke to your spouse in a way that you would never speak to a stranger?
14. What does a good presentation of an idea look like to you?
15. What makes you more receptive to hearing what another person has to say?

Call to Action

Try giving a message with a destructive tone here are the statements:

- *Have you made dinner yet?*
- *We need to pay the credit card bill.*

- *What did your mom say about our new house?*

Now let's practice those same statements with a more loving, and gentle tone.

CHAPTER FOUR - TIMEOUT TOOL

The Chase

A heated discussion needs resolution, and it must be Done Right Now! Only it doesn't. The desire for closure coupled with a spiritual desire to "not let the sun go down on one's anger," creates a scenario fraught with tension. Usually, one marriage partner wants to solve the issue right away and chases the other spouse around demanding an answer. Meanwhile, the other spouse wants to be removed from the situation and shut down the argument altogether. Expediency often comes from the enemy, like a bad infomercial: "You must act now!" Satan pushes the immediate and tries to keep us from going to the Father and seeking His will, in His time, in His way. But what if we slowed it down a bit? Afterall, biblical history has chronicled many instances where quick isn't always best.

❖ Sarah introduced her quick solution for an heir, instead of waiting for the miracle of God's provision (Genesis 16).

❖ Jobs' friends offered quick assessments and solutions instead of bowing their knee to God's process for suffering (Book of Job).

❖ King Saul offered a quick disobedient sacrifice out of fear, instead of waiting for Samuel to bless the battle (1 Samuel 13).

❖ David offered a quick solution to hide his sin by killing an innocent man instead of repenting and falling on the mercy of God (2 Samuel 11).

❖   Peter sliced off the ear of the Centurion's slave coming to capture Jesus instead of surrendering to God's perfect plan for salvation (Matthew 26:51).

❖   Perhaps the hastiest decision ever made was Eve's decision to believe Satan when he offered a counter belief about the goodness of God. Eve could have approached God directly (Genesis 3).

What exactly are the benefits of slowing down when conflicts arise? We have time for the information to come out. We have time for God to work on us and our spouse. We allow time for emotional temperature to adjust, and cooler heads to prevail. We can rely upon God's intervention with his unlimited resources, instead of bypassing God with our man-made remedies.

Following God means that we surrender our ways to his way. We follow, not lead. We bow, not demand. We seek first the kingdom of God; we wait upon the Lord to renew our strength. This replaces the desire for instant answers and temporal gratification found in *The Chase*.

When I am counseling couples about *The Chase*, it's only a matter of time when one of the spouses quotes Ephesians 4:26,

> *"Be angry, and yet do not sin; do not let the sun go down on your anger,"*

Many will view this verse as a time clock with the alarm set for midnight. But when looking at the context of the passage, they might be surprised. Paul is teaching the Church of Ephesus about Christian living and how it looks very different from the lifestyle of the unbeliever. Paul is not condemning anger; anger is not always a sin. Anger can be justified. We even see Jesus angry at times in the New Testament. This passage isn't about a deadline for conflict resolution, rather it's a mandate for the one who is angry. Hebrews 12:15 helps clear things up a bit,

> *"See to it that no one comes short of the grace of God; that no root of bitterness springing up causes trouble, and by it many*

be defiled."

In other words, you can be angry, but don't allow it to fester overnight. That type of response gives the enemy time to work what might be righteous anger into a bitter anger, one that leads to trouble and defilement. The Merium Webster Dictionary defines defile as: "to corrupt the purity or perfection of something." In this case, bitterness defiles the perfect idea God has for marriage.

So, what is the proper response, if not forced confrontation? In Romans 12:17-19 we receive clarity:

> *"Never pay back evil for evil to anyone. Respect what is right in the sight of all men. If possible, so far as it depends on you, be at peace with all men. Never take your own revenge, beloved, but leave room for the wrath of God, for it is written, "Vengeance is Mine, I will repay," says the Lord."*

The mandate to "not let the sun go down on your anger" is a message for the angry person, and an admonition to make sure his or her frustration of the situation isn't brought into the next day, but left at the feet of God who, in his time, will judge fairly. Not only is *The Chase* not biblical, but it eventually leads to two bad outcomes, both of which hurt the relationship by inflicting Emotional Scar Tissue.

Bad Outcome #1 Taking the Hit

The argument is going nowhere. You are dizzy with the circular discussion which has become a pattern, and you are tired. The thing you used to care about so deeply has been sucked out of you. You just want it to stop. Besides, you've danced to this song before, and it never ends up in your favor anyway. "I was wrong, we will do it your way!" you shout and make an exit stage right.

The history of Taking the Hit is easy to follow. One of the spouses might be an excellent orator, a great persuader, or verbally insistent, but also has no desire to entertain another viewpoint. When the opposing spouse lacks the opportunity for self-expression, to disagree, or sees the outcome as hopeless, he or she takes the hit and concedes, or retreats from the discussion altogether.

When this scenario is repeated time and again, trust is broken, and problem solving is seen as a total waste of time. The solution for one spouse is to speed up the process by always assuming blame and never engaging in difficult conversations. This leads to the couple assigning bad motives to one other; one for wanting to engage in unfruitful debate, and the other for being ambivalent in the relationship. This creates Emotional Scar Tissue which usually leads to emotional divorce.

Bad Outcome #2 Going Nuclear

The discussion between you and your spouse regarding a decision might seem to be going well as you introduce logical statements and crucial details, but then your spouse, who wants out of the conversation, will make a harsh statement that is very hurtful. The words are so damaging the discussion ends full stop. The spouse who delivered the bomb may believe the discussion has been shut down and the battle is over or even won. But this too doesn't solve the problem at all but introduces future problems.

Sure, the apology might come later, but when going nuclear is inflicted time and again, the spouse will develop deep emotional scar tissue and no longer believes the apology. Going nuclear in the form of insults, name calling, or degradation, destroys a person's self-worth. It's possible the person eventually begins to believe those cruel words and integrate them into his or her identity.

Eventually, for the sake of self-preservation, the offended person will permanently disengage. The only other option is to metaphorically *hit back harder*. That might work in a semi- hostile relationship but is destructive in a marriage. Repeatedly using the nuclear option to stop a discussion will eventually end the marriage.

These two solutions, *Taking the Hit* and *Going Nuclear*, are typical reactive responses when a couple is in *The Chase*. But what if you have an alternative? One that allows each person a voice at the table where he or she can be respected and heard. In my years of counseling I have introduced a tool that has changed the way many couples handle conflict. It's a practical tool that lowers the emotional temperature, slows down the process, and allows time for God's word to influence the conversation. It creates a united front by binding together the strands that God has joined.

The Timeout

When I use the term Timeout in the context of marriage, couples immediately imagine a scenario where one spouse banishes the other to a timeout chair in the corner of the kitchen. This is not that. Rather, timeout is a tool that couples can practice when a discussion becomes heated or out of control. Timeout occurs when both husband and wife go to different locations in the house where they can process what just occurred; But it's more than that; simply being alone to cool down will not necessarily mean that upon returning the bell will ring and round two begins. There must be a plan. When this Timeout Tool is practiced, couples find it minimizes the opportunity for emotional scar tissue to be inflicted upon each other. Let me lay out the process step by step.

Step 1

When you get a sense that the conversation is getting heated you say to your spouse, "Because I love you, I ask that we take a timeout right now, so we do not damage our relationship." Then retreat to separate places around the house. The goal is to find a space in the home where you would not be able to hear the other person if they spoke out loud. Additionally, children need to be insulated from hearing both parents. Once isolated, share with God your feelings on the matter at hand. As you share, keep these two thoughts in mind, God deserves your respect, and your spouse is God's child, whom He loves. You will know this step is complete when you have shared all your thoughts on the matter and are beginning to feel calmer. This may take 15-30 minutes. Now you are ready for step two.

Step 2

Remain in your isolated place and ask God three questions:
Question #1 What behaviors am I exhibiting that are escalating the conflict?

This is where God gently reminds us of our brokenness. Realize this conflict might be triggering trust or abandonment issues or something else entirely. Since God knows us, he is aware how our hang ups are negatively impacting the other person. We need to know these too, to avoid reacting the same way each time conflicts arise.

Question #2 *What I can do differently next time a similar situation arises like this?*

Be detailed about what you are going to do differently the next time this type of situation arises. This takes into consideration your spouse's brokenness regarding this issue.

Question #3 Ask God if there are other issues that have not been addressed.

Realize that sometimes the conflict at hand is only the tip of the iceberg and deeper issues are present. This stage is done when you have ideas of why you are having conflict, and what you can do differently the next time. Now you are ready for step three.

Step 3

Still in isolation, ask God how you can share your thoughts and ideas God revealed in step two in a gentle and loving way. Ask for God to be glorified in the way you speak to your spouse. Begin praying that your spouse can receive what you are going to share. When you are calm and at peace, let your spouse know that you are ready to meet. Then wait. Your spouse may need more time to process. Continue in prayer until you both can begin step four.

Step 4

As you come together you can calmly discuss the solutions to the conflict. Avoid statements like, "When you made that comment I was angry," and "I was hurt when you did this," and, "I did this behavior because I was angry at you." All those phrases will escalate the situation.

The husband speaks first. He has been chosen by God to be the leader and is responsible for his household. He asks his wife yes or no questions to clarify why she was angry. For example, "Were you angry when I came home late?" The husband shares his plan going forward to remedy the situation. The husband then apologies for his part in the conflict. He then addresses any other issues that God has revealed to him during his time of isolation. He asks yes or no questions for clarification and again offers the solution and apologies. The reason for limited input from the wife is to deter the situation from escalating back to pre-timeout level.

Next it is the wife's turn. She is to repeat the same scenario by asking questions for clarification, offering solutions, and apologizing for her part in the conflict.

This model works because it is hard to stay mad at a person when he or she is taking responsibility, offering solutions, and apologizing for his or her part in the conflict. Best of all the person feels heard. The goal is for each person to listen and be obedient to God, by discarding *The Chase*, and instead, taking active steps for better communication. Realize this model works with everyday communication problems that can be addressed with these techniques. However, major behavioral health issues such as addictions, infidelity, trauma, and domestic violence matters need professional intervention. My married couples have found that the *Timeout Tool* drastically reduces emotional scar tissue and presents a plan for de-escalation, allowing them a space for respectful discussion as God Intends.

Questions

1. Are you usually the chaser or the one being chased when you and your spouse are having an argument?
2. What are the benefits of slowing down when conflicts arise?
3. Have you ever gone to bed angry? What was your sleep like?
4. What happened when you returned to the previous discussion? Was it peaceful or more resentful?
5. Have you ever used your righteous anger to seek revenge?
6. What would happen if you placed problems at God's feet before you go to bed?
7. Have you ever *Taken the Hit* just to stop the discussion and have temporary peace?
8. Have you ever felt trapped in the martyr role?
9. If you always win a discussion because the other person concedes, do you feel more or less connected to that person?
10. What do you believe are the motives the other person has when engaging in the discussion?
11. Have you ever gone nuclear?
12. If you went nuclear and then apologized, what was the response from your spouse?
13. How does going nuclear change the relationship?
14. What does it look like when both people go nuclear?
15. Where is your possible quiet place to retreat to?
16. Do you have behaviors that escalate a conflict?
17. What are other responses you could exhibit that could cool the conflict?
18. Have you ever prayed for your spouse before?
19. Have you ever prayed for your spouse when you are angry at him or her? Why or why not?
20. How would praying for your spouse be helpful?
21. Why is it important for the husband to go first?

22. What is God's expectation for the husband?
23. How does taking turns create an orderly and less hostile environment?
24. Why are apologies important?

Call to Action

Make an appointment with your spouse and decide your code word and rules about how to implement timeout before you need it. Put the rules on paper and commit to practicing the Timeout Tool.

CHAPTER FIVE – LISTENING TOOL

I Can't Hear You

How many times have you been in a conversation with someone and realized you have no idea what he or she is talking about? Somewhere along the way you checked out. You can blame distractions like scrolling the phone during the conversation or children acting out, but regardless, communication was interrupted.

You are not alone, listening well to others has become a lost art. There are unofficial rules to listening but unfortunately most people are not in compliance. For example, in a conversation the speaker is allotted time to express an idea or opinion in the best way possible. The speaker must be conscious of speaking clearly and concisely, with an understandable vocabulary, a correct level of loudness, and with proper civility given to the one receiving the message. The listener also has rules to follow by maintaining eye contact (if in person) and focusing on the words spoken. The listener is to remain focused on hearing the words and stay silent by not interrupting until the speaker has finished.

There are many challenges to conversing correctly for both the listener and the speaker. For the listener there is the temptation to assume what the speaker will say and mentally fill in those words instead of what is actually being spoken. The listener might struggle to stay focused, allowing the mind to wander onto what he or she wants to say next. The speaker too might be challenged and struggle to find the correct word that adequately gets the message across. The speaker might incorrectly assume the listener possesses information and leave out pertinent details. Regardless of being the speaker or listener, when people don't listen to each other communication fails.

In a marriage, not listening or hearing the other person correctly creates problems. Often bad listening skills make the spouse feel disrespected, shuts down future communication, devalues the worth of the speaker, and eventually erodes all discussions in the relationship.

There is more to lose, however, than just words. The inability to listen sets you at a disadvantage for negotiation. You miss key elements where you and your spouse are on the same page; areas where you are willing to compromise. It's impossible to reach a resolution if you don't have the key facts in hand.

When couples come to my office with combative communication scenarios it is usually due to non-productive listening practices. This failure to communicate can be remedied by practicing active listening skills. I introduce to couples a tool that gets them into a healthy discussion pattern, it's called the Listening Game. Here are the rules:

1. Pick a topic that is not consequential in your relationship, a few suggestions might be your favorite fast food, a funny childhood memory, a book you've recently read.
2. Person A shares the topic while Person B just listens, no responding, no questions, no judgments just listening.
3. Person B then relates back to Person A what he or she heard with as many details as possible.
4. Person A confirms or shares what is missing from the story.
5. Now switch places and proceed accordingly.

The purpose of this little game is to expose areas where communication might be incomplete or broken in a low stakes' scenario, while providing a method for practicing good listening skills. Then, after practicing this tool with success, it's time to move onto more meaty discussions. Instead of pretending to listen, a couple can skillfully maneuver family topics.

Ears But Don't Hear

The Bible has a lot to say about good and bad communication and what active listening should look like. In James 1:19, we learn the process of good listening.

"This you know, my beloved brethren. But everyone must be quick to hear, slow to speak and slow to anger."

In Proverbs we are given bad examples of communication. In Proverbs 18:13,

"He who gives an answer before he hears, It is folly and shame to him."

and in Proverbs 18:2,

"A fool does not delight in understanding, But only in revealing his own mind."

In that verse in particular, we are shown a person who has no interest in communication but merely espousing his or her own opinions. A person like that isn't given a good outcome as we read in Proverbs 29:20,

"Do you see a man who is hasty in his words? There is more hope for a fool than for him."

Through the gospels Jesus is quoted as saying, "Whoever has ears to hear let them hear." Jesus isn't saying that people don't possess physical ears, he is saying that even when the people hear words, they don't always listen. In Matthew 13:13 he explained,

"This is why I speak to them in parables: Though seeing, they do not see; though hearing, they do not hear or understand."

Jesus was rebuking a crowd who were unable to truly listen and comprehend his teachings in order to receive the good news preached.

This model of listening to understand is crucial in a marriage. It is what sets apart a marriage where both feel heard and respected, from those that feel alienated and eventually estranged. Practicing the Listening Tool will build emotional intimacy in your relationship and protect it from the enemy who is always looking for a weakness in understanding.

Questions

1. Have you ever been in a conversation and suddenly found you have no idea what was being said?
2. What are the rules for speaking?
3. What are the rules for listening?
4. How can you personally become a good speaker and a good listener?
5. Do you remember a time when you struggled to be a good listener? A good speaker?
6. Why do you think listening is so difficult?
7. Think about someone who is purchasing a car or a new house, why is it important to have all the facts before making an important decision?
8. Predict right now how well you think you will perform in the Listening Tool?
9. How difficult is it to have a conversation with someone who does all the talking? Why is it difficult?
10. The word hasty means "acting too quickly." When can responding too quickly be a problem in communication?
11. How can Satan use poor listening skills to sideline relationships?

Call to Action

Practice the Listening Tool right now beginning with an easy topic. Now practice the Listening Tool again on a topic more challenging and personal.

CHAPTER SIX – COMPROMISE TOOL

The Sauce

One of our son's favorite homemade dinners is Spaghetti. He loves how my wife makes the sauce. I've watched her chop up the garlic and onions and add Italian seasonings. But the real secret is time. How weird would it be if she quickly mixed up all the raw ingredients, stirred it around, and plopped it on some noodles? Rather, it's the time simmering that allows all the ingredients to incorporate and become something else, something better.

The same is true in communication. Couples who have participated in the Listening Tool in the previous chapter, now have the raw ingredients for good communication like clarity, patience, and understanding. Both know what the other thinks and wants, but it would be foolish to jump ahead into a quick decision. It would be a bitter pasta sauce with loose ideas floating around without a purpose. Yet, many couples try to strong-arm the other to make a quick decision before dinner is ready. This push for a premature decision ends up causing regret.

There is a term in the sales industry called buyer's remorse. Whether it's a car, a cute handbag or an expensive dinner, the hype doesn't live up to the desired experience. One typical reason for the disappointment is because the decision was made in haste. You didn't take time to shop for other cars. You've realized that handbag comes with a hefty credit card bill. The meal costs you several points on your diet plan. Likewise, a person who is pushed into a decision before having time to weigh the cost is left feeling coerced, like a bad deal was made. This leads to bitterness. In a healthy marriage, it's important for a couple to eventually come to a consensus by compromise.

Not Easy

In case you think compromise is easy, it's not. If you are a history buff you might remember the United States Constitution almost ceased to exist, until The Great Compromise of 1787. As a new country, larger states believed each state's representation should be according to population. This seemed unfair to states with a smaller population who would be at a disadvantage for representation. The debates were so fierce the Constitution was close to being tossed out. The compromise was to create two houses elected by the people: The House of Representatives would be represented by population, and The Senate would have two representatives regardless of the population. Under these concessions the Constitution was signed and ratified.

In a marriage compromise is crucial. My Compromise Tool teaches couples how to remain at the table until an agreement is achieved. Just like a slow cooked sauce, there must be significant time for each spouse to contemplate. Contemplation is spiritual. It's a place to meet God and seek his discernment for the task at hand. It's a place where godly wisdom, not ego, needs to decide what is best. This might mean considering each other's strengths and weakness as a guide for moving forward, not a power tool to wield over one another.

We have a funny joke in our marriage; my wife Lynne is the risk-taker and the idea person, and it's my job to rain on her parade. At first this caused conflict in our marriage. She believed I only wanted to stymie all her suggestions, but over the years she has come to rely upon my 'glass half empty' approach to our decision-making process. The grace she has given me in expressing my hesitations has saved us from some bad decisions. Likewise, I rely on her to continue delivering good ideas; many have brought us good opportunities and blessings.

In my counseling experience, when one person tries to rush or shame the other into a decision, two things occur. First, mistakes are made, and blame becomes rampant. "If you hadn't pressured me into that decision this would have never happened." Second, one person takes the role of the martyr. "I guess I'll give up everything I want in order for you to be happy." Neither response is healthy. There is great power and ownership, however, when a couple has reached a conclusion together, taking each other's concerns and wishes into mind. It fosters maturity where each person must give up and gain something.

The Highway

Explanation of these tools, the Listening Tool and the Compromise Tool, wouldn't be complete without talking about scenarios when a spouse is not willing to negotiate at all. This is referred to as, "my way or the highway" meaning, either get on my path or get out.

This type of response creates a stalemate where neither person will give, and the possibility for agreement or decision is lost. In this situation, it's important to realize that something else is taking over. Resistance has a source, and signals hurt. It might be due to past experiences or involve fear of the unknown. What I do know is that when couples fall into this pattern of communication by insisting on one's own way, eventually passive aggressive solutions begin to take root, with each person acting out in their own perceived best interest.

Before any couple can move forward with good communication, there must be a safe place to share their fears. And these fears need to be respected. This can be possible with active listening, but remember the wall is there for a reason, and great care needs to be given before moving forward. For some this process may seem grueling, but the process itself builds intimacy and understanding into the marriage. Often trauma must be dealt with, or the individual struggling to make the decision might see compromise as another way to be taken advantage of.

All people have history. It takes both the Listening Tool

and the Compromise Tool to work through decisions that might look simple on the outside, but are in fact, deeply rooted in pain or uncertainty. It is by God's strength that we can maneuver gracefully through the difficulties in each other's life. It is because of our love and commitment to each other that we take the time necessary to love the other person through these challenges. Ecclesiastes 4:9-10 says,

"Two are better than one because they have a good return for their labor. For if either of them falls, the one will lift up his companion. But woe to the one who falls when there is not another to lift him up."

It is true that we are on a highway, but walking the path together on one road offers many benefits. There is protection from bad decisions, peace in a relationship built upon mutual respect, and joy from the Lord who is our strength. It's true,

"a cord of three strands is not quickly torn apart." - *Ecclesiastics 4:12*

Questions

1. What was one rash decision that you later regretted?
2. When have you pushed someone into a decision? What was the outcome?
3. Can you share an idea at first you weren't on board with, but the other person kept pushing it? How did that make you feel?
4. Name a time when your spouse gave you time to think about a decision. What was the result?
5. How does taking time to process a decision benefit you as a couple?
6. Why is compromise so difficult?
7. How do you and your spouse differ when it comes to decision making?
8. Have you ever felt embarrassed to share the real reason you are against a decision?
9. How does *my way or the highway* thinking disrupt good decision making as a couple?
10. How does compromise benefit you as a couple?
11. How are you and your spouse stronger together?

Call to Action

Set a calendar appointment time when you and your spouse can meet to revisit a decision that needs time to simmer. During the waiting process ask God for wisdom and insight about the decision.

CHAPTER SEVEN
- WINNING

When two boxers go at it in the ring, there is only one winner. There are three ways to win: by knockout, when the boxer is knocked down and unable to get up within ten seconds; by technical knockout, where the boxer is unable to fight because of injury or exhaustion; and by decision, when the winner is determined by the judges' scorecards after a fight continues until the end. One thing is for sure; someone must lose.

When it comes to marriage, couples that refuse to learn healthy communication skills behave like boxers in a ring. There is an unhealthy satisfaction in *taking the other down* or *showing him or her who's really in charge*, that is until someone throws in the towel. Jesus spoke about it in Mark chapter 10. He called it *hardness of heart*. In Mark 10:5-8, we read about some Pharisees approaching Jesus, asking about divorce if a woman displeased her husband. Jesus was quick to clarify the unfortunate necessity of this practice and reminded them of God's intention for marriage.

> *"But Jesus said to them, "Because of your hardness of heart he wrote you this commandment. But from the beginning of creation, God made them male and female. For this reason a man shall leave his father and mother and the two shall become one flesh; so they are no longer two, but one flesh. What therefore God has joined together, let no man separate."*

Hard Hearts

Mankind through his hard heart is the one who desecrates what God has created to be holy and good. Hardness of heart is spoken of when describing the Israelites who were disobedient in the desert with Moses, keeping a generation of them from entering the Promised Land:

> " Therefore, as the Holy Spirit says: Today, if you hear his voice, Do not harden your hearts as when they provoked Me, As in the day of trial in the wilderness, Where your fathers tried Me by testing Me, And saw My works for forty years. Therefore, I was angry with this generation, And said, 'They always go astray in their heart, And they did not know My ways'; As I swore in My wrath, They shall not enter My rest.'" - Hebrews 3:7-11.

It is the same hardness of heart described in scripture when the unbeliever is darkened in understanding, keeping him or her separated from God.

> So this I say, and affirm together with the Lord, that you walk no longer just as the Gentiles also walk, in the futility of their mind, being darkened in their understanding, excluded from the life of God because of the ignorance that is in them, because of the hardness of their heart; - Ephesians 4:17-18.

Truly, this is the same hardness of heart that keeps couples from living as one flesh as God intended. But there is hope. Thankfully, that same hardness of heart can be transformed by God's supernatural power. Ezekiel 36:26-28 states:

> "Moreover, I will give you a new heart and put a new spirit within you; and I will remove the heart of stone from your flesh and give you a heart of flesh. I will put My Spirit within you and cause you to walk in My statutes, and you will be careful to observe My ordinances. You will live in the land that I gave to your forefathers; so you will be My people, and I will be your God."

The process of softening the heart is imperative for a successful marriage. Each of the tools I've shared requires a heart transformation for both husband and wife.

A New Beginning

Before any tools are practiced, there must be a commitment from each to avoid giving EMOTIONAL SCAR TISSUE (as discussed in Chapter One). There needs to be trust that communication, even conflict, is safe. Success is not defined as winning at any cost or to make a point, but what the team needs to succeed. Improper responses like belittling, name calling, or aggressive behavior are counterproductive and shut down communication. Forgiving the individual for past infractions is also mandatory for the relationship to move forward and thrive.

The WAITING TOOL (Chapter Two) reminds us to respect the process of discovery before forming an opinion and responding by waiting until all information is disclosed. While waiting, it's important to practice love with patience and kindness, while keeping oneself from anger and other destructive reactions.

There is a softening of how the message itself is delivered In the DELIVERY TOOL (Discussed in Chapter Three). Gentleness and timing become the hallmark of good communication, as you understand the person well enough to effectively communicate. You've acquired the special language you share as a couple. Words spoken are measured in tone with good timing and communicated with respect, as the listener tries to process new or difficult information.

The TIMEOUT TOOL (Chapter Four) offers a process for cultivating a soft heart by avoiding heated moments, and allotting time for reflection and seeking the heart of God on the matter at hand. You've learned how to take a break when emotions are running so strong that you might be tempted to deliver emotional scar tissue. This allows an avenue for anger but offers an opportunity to deal with it later in a constructive way.

The LISTENING TOOL (Chapter Five) puts great value upon how to hear what the other person is truly saying. Our hard heart is broken when we realize how often we speak first and listen later.

Instead, we learn a discipline that focuses on hearing the other person out, elevating his or her words, instead of solely focusing on our own opinions.

In the COMPROMISE TOOL (Chapter Six) couples have the time necessary to incorporate solutions together by reaching a compromise that both can live with. Instead of seeing the other as an impediment to your goal, your spouse is seen as an asset bringing another perspective that protects you as a couple over time.

These tools only work when there is a foundational relationship with God, otherwise it is a tool that can be misused and misinterpreted. God is the one who wants us to have healthy relationships because it glorifies Him and is best for His creation. But it's difficult to change without the Holy Spirit to guide us through the various tools and give us the strength to be patient and calm, especially when our flesh is crying out otherwise. The success of communication is only possible through God's power when you invite Christ into your marriage and into your life. It's a witness to the world that they will know us by our love one for another.

Investment

Let's move on from the earlier boxing match metaphor. Allow me to share a less hostile sport: golf. You may have heard the term playing the short game in golf. It refers to the aspect of the game that involves hitting a short to medium distance usually within 100 yards of the green. It's the hardest to play, and quite often where the most strokes are lost. In other words, it takes practice, lots of practice. Many of the couples I see want to ignore their short game and the time and precision it takes to build a healthy relationship.

But for those who are committed to the wedding day promise made to each other, their families, and to God, they have agreed to more than happily ever after, you have agreed to the process. The journey to the cross is not an easy one; it's fraught with challenges, and disappointments, but also blessings.

I'm reminded of the wedding or party favor my bride and I gave to those who attended our ceremony so many years ago; It was a Bible bookmark. On it was written John 15:5:

"I am the vine, you are the branches; he who abides in Me and I in him, he bears much fruit, for apart from Me you can do nothing."

At that time, we didn't fully appreciate the magnitude of those words in relation to our marriage. The success or failure of our relationship was fully dependent upon our remaining connected to the one who sustains us. Earlier in the same chapter John writes about the Lord needing to prune us so that we can be fruitful. Marriage is the perfect covenant relationship profitable for pruning. It's where we learn about our rough branches and ideas that need to be clipped or sometimes cut off altogether; it is where we learn how to gently guide each other toward holiness.

RESOURCES

PeteThompson.org

How Anxiety Destroyed King Saul by Pete Thompson LCSW & Lynne Thompson

While We Wait A Devotional For Those Who Love The Prodigal by Lynne Thompson

Focus On The Family Christian Counselors Network

PRAYER TO ACCEPT JESUS

If you have never asked the Savior, Christ Jesus, into your life, today can be your day to receive God's greatest gift.

Dear God,

I have sinned against you and against others, and I could never be good enough to enter Your Kingdom. Please forgive me. Thank you for sending Your Son, Jesus, to die on the cross for my sins, and to pay my way into heaven. I now give my life over to You as a living sacrifice. I want to do things Your way. Come into me, Holy Spirit, and direct my path in the way everlasting.

Amen.

OTHER WORKS BY PETE & LYNNE THOMPSON

Books for Purposeful Living Today

Visit: https://www.petethompson.org/shop/

While We Wait: A Devotion for Those Who Love the Prodigal

In her book, Lynne Thompson offers a devotional filled with inspirational stories on how to keep our eyes on what's important, as we walk this holy journey, waiting for our prodigals to come home. Each day offers a biblically focused story, a prayer, a biblical verse for encouragement, and an activity to help you move forward during this trial. Hope is waiting.

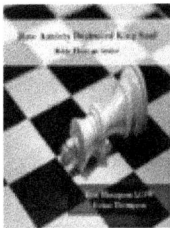

How Anxiety Destroyed King Saul

Pete and Lynne Thompson invite you to sit-in on three counseling sessions featuring a biblical character who needed healing from this very condition. With over 35 years in the mental health field, Pete offers biblical insight for this challenging, yet treatable mental health issue.

Wag The Mouth

Can geeks become the most popular people on campus? They can if Tori Sanchez is in charge! Tori has a plan for creating a 'geek-friendly' school, but it's going to take a cow, some risk, and maybe just a little romance. It's time for the rise of the Geek Elite!

Wag The Teacher
Can the coolest teacher on campus be transformed into a geek? Tori is back again, and this time tries her hand at matchmaking. Her plan includes a crazy makeover for one single mom, and geek school for one lucky teacher.

READY FOR A SIMPLE REMODEL?

Practice easy to use tools for good communication

Pete & Lynne Thompson introduce five communication tools that will bring peace and healing to your relationship. It's not too late to honor God with the way you speak to the people you care about.

Pete Thompson is a Licensed Clinical Social Worker (LCSW) practicing for over thirty-eight years. He runs Pete Thompson Christian Counseling in North Texas, and helps clients throughout the USA and Internationally by telehealth. Pete combines a cognitive behavioral approach with the infinite resources of knowledge found in God's Holy Word, the Bible.

Lynne Thompson is author of The *Official Soccer Mom Devotional* (Regal Books). She is also known for her 'Soccer Mom Moments' broadcasted throughout the United States and Canada on Focus on the Family's Weekend radio show. Her favorite role is wife to Pete, and mother to their two adult children.

You can reach Pete & Lynne at:
PeteThompson.org

ISBN 979-8-9994946-0-3

9 798999 494603

90000>

·ww.ingramcontent.com/pod-product-compliance
·htning Source LLC
·bersburg PA
·071853020426
·CB00007B/1988